# CLASS FAVORITES
## Take-to School Treats
## for Every Holiday

■ **easy to make** ■ **easy to carry** ■ **easy to eat**

## BY
## LEIGH ANN MICHAEL

ISBN: 0-9675634-0-2

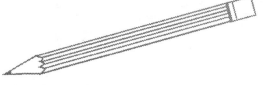

To order additional copies, please write to:

Class Favorites
1601 Lovers Lane
Booneville, MS 38829
Phone: 601/728-7665  Fax: 601/728-4422


First Printing May, 2000
Second Printing July, 2001

cookbook
resources.
541 Doubletree Drive
Highland Village, TX 75067
972/317-0245
www.cookbookresources.com

# CONTENTS

# ACKNOWLEDGEMENTS

I want to thank my husband, Randy and our four lovely, active daughters, Ashleigh, Sara Beth, Mallory and Gracie for helping me taste test these recipes and for being my inspiration in everything I do. I love you all!

# INTRODUCTION

Class Favorites comes from my experiences as a wife and mother, with four very busy, school aged girls. Each girl was involved in special activities, requiring sweet treats, or a party, for celebrating victories, holidays, etc. With so much going on, we soon became tired of the same old party treats. All the moms served the same desserts, and the kids wanted something new. I was running out of time and out of ideas, spending too much time worrying about how to get everything done. I wrote Class Favorites as a way of organizing my favorite recipes, and keeping my easy dessert ideas in one place. The book is organized by school holidays for easy reference, but most recipes can be made for any occasion.

I know you've been here: your child announces at 7PM that he or she has to have a treat for a school or sports function the next day — and you panic. Or, you find out at a 5PM staff meeting that you're supposed to bring the office birthday treat to lunch the next day. Don't panic — you now have a method of saving your sanity — and a way to offer your friends and your children something fun to eat. This is a real life rescue system for busy moms (and dads) who need to make take-to-school treats at the last minute. You can make any of these recipes on a busy schedule. Just a little planning, basic on-hand ingredients and about a half-hour of your time is all you'll need.

None of these recipes are difficult to make or to transport. Many can be taken to school or to the office in their baking pan or a plastic container. Frozen desserts are carried in their pie plate and punch can be taken in a large plastic jug. Cookies, candy and snack mixes are tasty and simple, and all travel well.

Not all the recipes are original, but they are our favorites and all have been adapted for preparation within a very busy schedule. Many of these recipes are simple enough to introduce children to baking — requiring very little adult supervision. Let a trusted teenager or babysitter entertain the kids in the kitchen while you're on a "rare" night out. Grandparents also will like this book because it gives them great tasting sweet ideas to prepare with their precious guests during a sleepover.

## Panic Free Pantry

Keep these basic ingredients in your cupboard (according to your tastes), and you can make most of the recipes in this book. You may have to run out to get milk or margarine, but the rest of these ingredients will keep in your cupboard until you need them.

2-3 boxes of cake mix, different flavors
2-3 cans of ready to spread frosting, different flavors
2-3 boxes of instant pudding (4 serving size)
2-3 boxes of flavored gelatin
1 package chopped pecans
Mini marshmallows
Canned pie filling
Semi-sweet chocolate chips
Peanut butter chips
Flaked coconut
Prepared graham cracker crust
Toppings for ice cream
Eagle brand sweetened condensed milk
Peanut butter
Pretzels
Peanuts
Frozen whipped topping

If you have 13 x 9-inch baking pan, a bundt pan, two cookie sheets and some basic cooking utensils, you're ready to go!

Enjoy!

Leigh Ann Michael

# AFTER SCHOOL TREATS

$2 + 2 = 4$

SCHOOL

# NOTES:

## ASHLEIGH'S CINNAMON TOAST

*This is the first thing my daughter
learned to make for herself.*

**Sliced white bread**

**Butter**

**Cinnamon**

**White sugar**

Preheat oven to 350°. Spread butter on bread. Sprinkle cinnamon on butter, then sprinkle sugar on top. Bake in a 350° oven until bread is toasted.

## MONKEY BREAD

**3 packages canned biscuits
(12 count)**

**1 ¾ cups sugar**

**1 ½ tablespoons cinnamon**

**1 ½ sticks butter**

Preheat oven to 350°. Quarter each biscuit. Place ¾ cup sugar and cinnamon into a plastic freezer bag. Place biscuits into plastic bag with sugar mix and roll or shake until coated. Place biscuit pieces into a greased bundt cake pan. Bring 1cup sugar and butter to a boil and pour over biscuits. Bake for 30-40 minutes in a 350° oven. Cool and dump cake out onto a serving plate. Great for breakfast. Kids can eat this with their fingers.

## CREAM CHEESE ROLLS

**2 packages crescent rolls**

**2 packages cream cheese
(8-ounce size)**

**1 ¼ cups sugar**

**1 stick butter**

**1 Teaspoon cinnamon**

**pie filling (optional) any flavor**

Preheat oven to 350°. Roll out 1 can of rolls. Place in a 13 × 9-inch baking dish. Mix cream cheese and 1 cup sugar until creamy. Spread on top of rolls. Place second can of rolls on top of cream cheese mixture. Melt butter and pour over rolls. Sprinkle with ¼ cup sugar and cinnamon. Bake in a 350° oven until rolls are well done. Don't let them burn.

Qq  Rr  Ss  Tt  Uu  Vv  Ww  Xx  Yy  Zz  1 2 3 4 5 6 7 8 9 10

## CHOCOLATE ROLLS

1 can crescent rolls
½ cup semi-sweet chocolate chips
confectioner's sugar

Preheat oven to 350°. Flatten rolls on ungreased cookie sheet. Sprinkle chips in the middle of each roll and fold into a triangle. Bake until light brown. Sprinkle with sugar.

## HEAVENLY CHOCOLATE DROPS

1 box devils food cake mix
2 eggs
½ cup oil
1 package semi-sweet chocolate chips

Preheat oven to 350°. Mix all ingredients. Drop by tablespoons onto an ungreased cookie sheet. Bake in a 350° oven for 10-12 minutes.

## SUGAR BISCUITS

1 can refrigerator biscuits
White sugar
Cooking oil

Deep fry biscuits until brown. Roll in sugar. Serve.

## WHITE NIBBLETS

1 pound white chocolate
1 cup peanuts
1 cup pretzel sticks

Melt white chocolate over medium heat. Stir in peanuts and pretzels until coated in chocolate. Spread on cookie sheet. Let stand until cool. Break into bite size pieces when firm.

Aa Bb Cc Dd Ee Ff Gg Hh Ii Jj Kk Ll Mm Nn Oo Pp

# S'MORES

*Everyone can make these –*

**Graham crackers**
**Chocolate bars**
**Marshmallows**

**P**lace candy bar on graham cracker, add marshmallows. Top with another graham cracker. These can be heated just slightly in the microwave (so chocolate and marshmallows are gooey) or cooked over a camp fire.

# ICE CREAM MUFFINS

**1 cup vanilla ice cream (softened)**
**1 cup self-rising flour**
**1 tablespoon butter**
**2 tablespoons sugar**
**1 cup fresh strawberries**

**P**reheat oven to 350°. In mixing bowl, mix ice cream, flour, butter and sugar. Add strawberries. Spoon into muffin cups. Bake in a 350° oven for 22-25 minutes. Top with a sprinkle of sugar.

# BUTTERSCOTCH COOKIES

**1 box butterscotch cake mix**
**2 eggs**
**½ cup oil**
**1 package butterscotch chips**
**½ cup pecans**

**P**reheat oven to 350°. Mix all ingredients. Drop by tablespoons onto an ungreased cookie sheet. Bake in a 350° oven for 10-12 minutes.

# CEREAL BALLS

1 cup peanut butter

1 cup confectioner's sugar

1 cup puffed rice cereal

3 tablespoons butter, melted

1 cup semi-sweet chocolate chips

1 ounce paraffin wax

**M**ix first four ingredients. Roll into 1-inch balls. Melt chocolate chips and paraffin wax together. Dip balls into chocolate mixture. Place on wax paper to cool. Balls will harden.

# DISAPPEARING MINI CHEESECUPS

1 box of cheesecake mix

vanilla wafers

1 can strawberry pie filling

**P**repare cheesecake according to package directions. Put 1 vanilla wafer into bottom of a muffin tin. Pour cheesecake mixture over wafer. Cool. Top with strawberry pie filling. These will not last long!

# RICE CEREAL SQUARES

Just in case you've been living on another planet and missed this one, here's the all time favorite kids snack!

4 tablespoons butter

4 cups marshmallows

5 cups rice cereal

**M**elt butter in a large saucepan over low heat. Add marshmallows and stir until melted. Cook for 2 minutes. Remove from heat. Add rice cereal. Spray a 13 x 9-inch pan with vegetable spray. Pour in cereal mix, press to the sides of the pan and cool.

Aa Bb Cc Dd Ee Ff Gg Hh Ii Jj Kk Ll Mm Nn Oo Pp

## DRESSED UP CEREAL SQUARES

**1 cup light corn syrup**
**1 cup sugar**
**1 cup peanut butter**
**4 cups corn flakes**
**4 cups cheerios**
**1 cup peanuts**

In large saucepan, melt first three ingredients. When smooth (do not boil or overcook), add last three ingredients. When well coated, pour into a buttered or sprayed 13 x 9-inch pan. Cool and cut into squares.

## ANTS IN THE SAND

**Graham crackers, crushed**
**Semi-sweet chocolate chips**

Mix crackers and chocolate chips in a zip-lock bag. Small children can carry this snack with them and not spill a crumb!

## ANTS ON A LOG

**Celery**
**Peanut butter**
**Chocolate chips or raisins**

Wash celery and cut into small logs. Spread peanut butter onto celery and top with chocolate chips or raisins.

## HAYSTACKS

**4 cups butterscotch chips**
**1 large can chow mein noodles**
**1 can peanuts**

Melt chips over low heat. Remove from heat and stir in noodles and peanuts. Drop by tablespoon onto waxed paper. Serve when cooled.

# PUPPY CHOW

1 cup smooth peanut butter

1 cup semi-sweet chocolate chips

8 cups Corn Chex cereal

2 cups confectioner's sugar

Melt peanut butter and chocolate chips over low heat. Add corn chex and mix until well coated. When coated, place in large plastic freezer bag with sugar. Shake until well coated. Can also use rice chex cereal.

# SAUSAGE ROLLS

Another standby that kids will pop into their mouths as fast as you can make them!

1 lb. sausage

4 cups shredded cheese

1 package crescent rolls

Preheat oven to 375°. Brown sausage and drain on paper towel. Separate rolls and flatten. Pour sausage into the widest part of the triangle and top with cheese. Roll up and pinch the sides. Bake in a 375° oven until lightly browned.

# HOLE IN ONE

Sliced white bread

Butter

Eggs

Salt and pepper to taste

Shredded cheddar cheese

Take one slice of bread. Tear out a hole in the middle of the bread and place bread in a buttered frying pan. Crack one egg and place in the hole in the bread. Fry until egg is cooked as you desire. Season with salt and pepper. Top with shredded cheese.

## HAM AND CHEESE SANDWICH

**1 package crescent dinner rolls**

**shredded cheddar cheese**

**cooked sliced ham**

**P**reheat oven to 350°. Unroll rolls. Place about 1 tablespoon each of ham and cheese in middle of each roll. Roll up and pinch sides to make a triangle. Bake in a 350° oven for 12-15 minutes until brown.

## QUICK TO EAT PIZZA SNACKS

**Ritz Crackers**

**Pizza Sauce**

**Shredded Mozzarella cheese**

**P**reheat oven to 350°. Place cracker, salt side down on cookie sheet. Spoon pizza sauce on cracker. Top with cheese. Place in oven until cheese melts. Serve warm. Add pepperoni, onions, cooked ground beer or mushrooms if you desire.

*Alternate:* Use a slice of bread, or a sliced bagel, instead of the cracker.

*Alternate:* Use biscuits as the pizza dough. Flatten biscuit, and add desired toppings. Bake in a 375° oven until cheese melts and biscuit is cooked.

## STAND BY TUNA FISH

*Another basic. This is so easy, kids can prepare with
a small amount of supervision.*

**3 hard boiled eggs (Mom needs to do this part)**

**2 tablespoons mayonnaise**

**1 can tuna (drained)**

**Small amount of salt and pepper to taste**

Chop eggs (can be done with a fork or table knife, to protect little fingers), add mayonnaise and drained tuna. Mix well. Add a small amount of salt and pepper to taste. Serve on crackers or toasted bread.

*Alternate:* You can also put in a teaspoon of pickle relish, if you like that sort of thing!

## PIGS IN A BLANKET

**1 package crescent rolls**

**American cheese slices, cut into thin strips**

**Mini party franks or sausage**

Unroll rolls and place weiners/sausage and cheese into center. Roll up. Bake in a 375° oven until slightly brown and cheese begins to melt.

## MALLORY'S PICK ME UP POTATO CHEESY

**Baking potatoes**

**1 stick butter or margarine (melted)**

**shredded cheddar cheese**

**bacon bits**

Preheat oven to 375°. Wash potatoes and slice lengthwise with skin still on. Place in a baking pan. Pour melted butter over potato. Bake in a 375° oven until tender. When potatoes are done, sprinkle with cheese and top with bacon bits. Put back into oven until cheese is melted. Great served with ranch dressing.

Aa Bb Cc Dd Ee Ff Gg Hh Ii Jj Kk Ll Mm Nn Oo Pp

## PAPA'S GRILLED CHEESE

2 slices of bread

1 slice cheese

butter

**P**lace cheese between bread. Melt butter in a frying pan. Place sandwich in butter and fry. Turn to brown both sides. (Papa makes this when the kids drop in to spend the night. They say Papa's grilled cheese is better than anyone's – including Ma's.)

## SAUSAGE MUFFINS

¼ lb. sausage, drained

3 ounces cream cheese

½ cup shredded cheddar cheese

1 cup biscuit mix

2 eggs

²/₃ cup milk

**P**reheat oven to 350°. Combine all ingredients in a large mixing bowl. Spoon into greased muffin tins. Bake in a 350° oven for 30-40 minutes. Check to make sure these don't burn on the top.

## CHEESE BUTTON SNACKS

1 cup cheddar cheese, shredded

¼ cup butter

½ cup whole wheat flour

**P**reheat oven to 350°. Mix all ingredients in a large bowl. Roll into small balls and place on a greased cookie sheets. Flatten to button size! Bake in a 350° oven for 10-15 minutes. Be careful not to let the edges burn.

# COLORFUL ICE CUBE POPS

### This is an old standby! The kids can make these.

**Kool Aid**
**Ice cube trays**

Prepare Kool Aid per package directions. Pour into ice cube trays and freeze.

*Alternate:* Cover ice cube tray with plastic wrap and insert a toothpick into each cube. These make great frozen ice treats – complete with a little handle!

*Alternate:* Use flavored ice cubes in your favorite punch instead of sherbet or ice cream.

# HALLOWEEN

**What is a monster's favorite cafeteria food?**

# NOTES:

Grave-y

## BUMP IN THE NIGHT
## GHOST CUPCAKES

**24 ready to eat cupcakes (any flavor)**

**Chocolate icing (unless your cupcakes already are iced)**

**24 Nutter Butter Cookies**

**Tube of chocolate decorator icing**

**White icing**

Top cupcakes with chocolate icing. Frost each cookie with white icing. Make ghost face on each cookie with decorator icing. Insert cookie into top of cupcake.

## BAT WINGS

**1 box cake mix (any flavor)**

**1 can ready to spread frosting (any flavor)**

**Small gum drops**

**Mini marshmallows**

**Fruit roll ups**

Prepare cupcakes according to package directions. Frost when cool. Make bats ears out of gumdrops. Use chocolate chips for eyes and mini marshmallows for teeth. Cut wings from fruit roll ups and place on each side of cupcake.

## SPOOKY SPIDER CUPCAKES

**1 box chocolate cake mix**

**Halloween cupcake liners**

**1 can ready to spread vanilla frosting**

**Red hots candy**

**Gumdrops**

**Black licorice**

**Chocolate sprinkles**

Prepare cupcakes according to package directions. Frost when cool. Use red hots candy for spider's eyes. Use a gumdrop for the nose and stick black licorice into the side of each cupcake to form spider's legs. Add a few chocolate sprinkles to the top of the cupcake for color.

## GRACIE'S GRAVEYARD CUPCAKES

1 box of your favorite cake mix (chocolate will make this look like dirt)

1 package chocolate pudding (instant) – or use ready made pudding cups

8-ounce Halloween paper drinking cups

Gummi worms

Coconut

Green food coloring

Prepare cupcakes according to package directions. Let cool. Mix pudding according to package directions. Place ¼ cup pudding in the bottom of each Halloween paper cup. Add cupcake on top of pudding. Spoon ¼ cup pudding on top of cupcake. Stick gummi worms into pudding so it looks like they're crawling out of the side. Top with green colored coconut to look like grass.

## MINI MUMMY MUFFINS

1 roll peanut butter cookie dough

1 bag miniature peanut butter cup candy

Preheat oven to 350°. Spray muffin tins with non-stick spray. Slice cookie dough and roll into small balls (about the size of a quarter). Drop into sprayed muffin tins. Bake in a 350° oven for 8-10 minutes. Remove from oven. Press a peanut butter cup into the center of each cookie. Remove muffin from tin (you'll have to run a knife around the edge to get it out of the pan). Cool thoroughly. Makes 36 mini-muffins.

## COOKIES WITH A NAME ON TOP

1 bag of fudge covered sandwich cookies

1 orange gel decorating tip

Have your child bring you a list of all the names of the kids in her class. Write each child's name on a cookie with the decorating tip. Kids love to see their name on a cookie. This is really quick and is always a hit.

Aa Bb Cc Dd Ee Ff Gg Hh Ii Jj Kk Ll Mm Nn Oo Pp

## SLIMY WORM CAKE

- **1 box chocolate cake mix**
- **1 package frosting (either a can of ready made or a boxed mix)**
- **2 packages gummi worms**
- **1 package Oreo sandwich cookies**

**P**repare cake and frosting per package directions. Frost cake. Crush oreo cookies (use a plastic sandwich bag and a rolling pin) and sprinkle on top of cake, so the cake looks like it's covered in dirt. Place gummi worms into frosting, so they look like their crawling out of the cake.

*Fast alternative:* Buy a cake that's already frosted. Then add cookies and worms.

## HALLOWEEN GREEN GOOEY BLOBS

- **1 stick butter**
- **1 bag (10-ounce) large marshmallows**
- **5 cups corn flake cereal**
- **2 teaspoons green food coloring**
- **M&M plain chocolate candy**

**M**elt butter in large saucepan. Add marshmallows and melt over low heat. Remove from heat. Add food coloring and mix. Add corn flakes and mix until well coated (should be bright green). Add M&M candy (put in what you like – just enough to make it colorful). Drop by teaspoons onto was paper. Serve when cool.

These are green, gooey and really great treats for the little goblins in your house.

## HAUNTED SQUARES

- **Graham crackers or plain crackers or Ritz crackers**
- **Canned cheese spread**
- **Chocolate sprinkles**

**S**pread cheese on crackers and top with sprinkles.

Qq  Rr  Ss  Tt  Uu  Vv  Ww  Xx  Yy  Zz  1 2 3 4 5 6 7 8 9 10

## CANDLE SALAD

**1 leaf of lettuce**
**1 slice of pineapple**
**1 banana**
**1 teaspoon mayonnaise or**
**salad dressing**
**large Maraschino cherry**

On a salad plate, place the leaf of lettuce. Please the slice of pineapple on top of the lettuce leaf. Trim the top and bottom of the banana so each end is flat and will stand up in the center of the pineapple. Top the banana with mayonnaise and then the cherry.

This was the first item I ever made in the kitchen when I was about 7 years olds. Some 47 years later and I still remember.

## TREMBLING TREATS

**3 tablespoons butter**
**3 cups mini marshmallows**
**1 can chow mein noodles**
**12-14 caramels**
**1 tablespoon water**
**2 tablespoons peanut butter**

Heat butter and marshmallows over low heat until smooth. Add chow mein noodles. Mix until noodles are covered. Drop by tablespoons onto waxed paper. Melt caramels and water over low heat. When smooth, add peanut butter. Mix well. Pour over noodle mixture. Let set and serve.

## EYEBALL COOKIES

**1 package chocolate covered**
**fudge sandwich cookies**
**1 can white frosting**
**Chocolate chips**
**Jelly beans**
**Red decorating gel**

Frost the middle of each cookie, leaving the outside edge bare. Place chocolate chips or jelly beans in the center of each cookie to make eyes. Use red gel for bloodshot.

Aa Bb Cc Dd Ee Ff Gg Hh Ii Jj Kk Ll Mm Nn Oo Pp

## ITSY BITSY SPIDER

1 box of large peanut butter
  cookies

1 can white frosting

Black jelly beans (large)

Red jelly beans (small)

Black licorice

Frost cookies. Place 2 jelly beans on top of cookie to make spider's body and head. Use red jelly beans for antennae and licorice pieces for legs. This is easy for kids to make themselves.

## QUICK GRAHAM TREATS

Graham crackers

Miniature marshmallows

Oreo flavored cereal or
  cookies

Preheat oven to 350°. Place graham crackers on cookie sheet. Top with white marshmallows. Then put either cereal or crushed oreo cookies on top of marshmallows. Bake until melted and lightly brown.

## FRIENDLY GHOST COOKIES

6-ounces vanilla flavored
  almond bark

1 package Nutter Butter
  cookies

Small black jelly beans

Melt almond bark in a small saucepan. Dip 2/3 of each cookie in melted candy. Shake off excess. Place on waxed paper. For eyes, cut jelly beans in half and place on frosted part of cookie for eyes. This is an easy to make recipe that your kids can do themselves, as long as you supervise melting the candy.

## THE GREAT PUMPKIN

1 roll of refrigerator sugar
   cookie dough

1 can of white frosting

orange food coloring

coconut

green food coloring

Roll cookie dough onto a pizza pan. Bake per package directions until golden brown. Mix frosting with orange food coloring. Frost entire cookie, except leave a small space at the top. Drop a few drops of green food coloring into coconut and spread on top of cookie for the stem. Carefully remove from the pan and place on a colorful platter.

## SPIDER WEB COOKIES

1 package (20-ounce)
   chocolate chip cookie
   dough

2 packages (8-ounce each)
   cream cheese

½ cup sugar

½ teaspoon vanilla

2 eggs

2 squares semi-sweet baking
   chocolate, melted

Preheat oven to 325°. Spread cookie dough in a buttered 12-inch baking pan. Mix cream cheese, sugar, and vanilla until sell blended. Add eggs and mix well. Pour over cookie dough. Bake at 325° for 15 minutes. Cool completely. Cut into squares. Drizzle melted chocolate over each cookie to make a spider web effect.

## CREEPY CRAWLY CREATURES

1 roll refrigerated peanut
   butter cookie dough

1 can white frosting

gum drops for eyes

cheese puffs for antenna

chocolate chips for nose

Slice dough and roll out to about 2½ - 3 inches in diameter. Bake per package directions, being careful not to let the cookies overbake. Cool completely. Frost with white frosting. Use red gumdrops for eyes, chocolate chips for nose and cheese puffs for antenna.

Aa Bb Cc Dd Ee Ff Gg Hh Ii Jj Kk Ll Mm Nn Oo P

## SCARY CAT COOKIES

1 cup crunchy peanut butter

½ cup water

2 eggs

1 box chocolate cake mix

1 package M&M candy baking bits

1 bag red hots

Preheat oven to 350°. Mix peanut butter, water and eggs. Add cake mix. Mix well. Form into balls and place on an ungreased cookie sheet. Flatten balls with a rolling pin or the bottom of a glass dipped in sugar. Pinch ear shapes at the top of each cookie. Add M&M bits for eyes and red hots for nose. Press fork into cookie for whiskers. Bake in a 350° oven for 8-10 minutes.

## HALLOWEEN CREAMY COOKIES

Ritz crackers

Creamy peanut butter

White chocolate – melted

Orange sprinkles

Take Ritz crackers and make a sandwich, using peanut butter as filling. Dip each sandwich into melted chocolate. Place on wax paper to let chocolate harden. Top with orange sprinkles.

## SPOOKY PALS

1 can refrigerated sugar cookie dough

Ghost cookie cutter

1 can ready to spread white frosting

Black jelly beans or chocolate chips

Roll cookie dough to ¼ inch thickness. Cut with ghost cookie cutter. Bake per package instructions. Frost when cool. Use candy for eyes.

Qq  Rr  Ss  Tt  Uu  Vv  Ww  Xx  Yy  Zz   1 2 3 4 5 6 7 8 9 10

## CANDY CORN POPCORN BALLS

**¼ cup butter**

**1 package mini marshmallows**

**1 package orange gelatin dessert**

**12 cups popped popcorn**

**1 ½ cups candy corn**

Melt butter and marshmallows in a medium saucepan. When melted, add gelatin. Pour marshmallow mixture over popped corn, adding candy corn. Stir until all is coated. Grease hands with margarine and shape into balls.

## CREEPY CRAWLY PRETZELS

**2 round crackers**

**2 teaspoons smooth peanut butter**

**8 small pretzel sticks**

**chocolate chips**

With the peanut butter, make a cracker sandwich. Insert 8 pretzel stick "legs" into filling. With a dab of peanut butter, place two chocolate chip eyes on top.

These look like they'll crawl off the plate. Kids will squeal when they see them!

## BOO SNACK MIX

**4 cups Halloween colored rice cereal**

**1 ½ cups mini marshmallows**

**1 cup semi-sweet chocolate chips**

Mix all ingredients in a large bowl. An easy sweet snack that kids can make in a flash.

Aa Bb Cc Dd Ee Ff Gg Hh Ii Jj Kk Ll Mm Nn Oo Pp

## SPIDER BITES

1 12-ounce package semi-sweet chocolate chips

1 can chow mein noodles

1 package M&M baking bits

Melt chocolate chips over low heat. Remove from heat. Stir in noodles. Drop by teaspoons onto wax paper. Place 2 M&M bits on each cookie for eyes.

## DUNKING CARAMEL APPLES

1 (14-ounce) package caramels

1 cup mini marshmallows

1 ½ tablespoons water

6 red apples

Colored sprinkles or candy corn for decorations

6 Halloween cupcake tins

6 wooden sticks

Melt caramels, marshmallows and water over low heat until completely melted. Insert a wooden stick into the end of each apple and dip into caramel mixture. Place in cupcake tins and push down to flatten the bottom. Decorate apples while still warm. Make a face with the candy, or use nuts or sprinkles.

## BLOOD SOAKED POPCORN!

Add red food coloring to butter while it's melting. Pour red butter over popcorn. Serve to your little vampires.

## BEWITCHING CRACKER SNACKS

Cheesecake flavored cream cheese spread

Graham crackers

Halloween sprinkles

Spread cream cheese on crackers. Top with sprinkles. Kids can make this one in a flash.

## WORM RING

1 cup gummi worms
1 bottle (2 liter) 7-up

**P**lace worms in the bottom of a bundt pan or ring mold. Fill with 7-up. Freeze overnight. Use in your favorite punch. Add more worms to the punch.

## SPOOKY PUNCH

2 packages cherry Kool Aid
1 quart unsweetened
   pineapple juice
2 quarts water
2 cups sugar
1 quart ginger ale
Crushed Ice

**M**ix all ingredients and serve immediately

## WITCH'S POTION

1 14.5 ounce can Eagle brand
   condensed milk
1 (46-ounce) can pineapple
   juice, chilled
1 2 liter bottle orange soda,
   chilled
1 pint orange sherbet

**S**tir milk, pineapple juice and orange soda in a punch bowl. Top with scoops of orange sherbet. (Can serve over crushed ice if desired.)

## WITCH'S BREW

3 pints grape juice
1 ½ pints club soda
grapes – seedless
apples

**M**ix grape juice and soda in a pitcher. Cut apples into small chunks. Pour into punch bowl. Add fruit at the last minute. The punch looks like there are eyes and teeth floating in the bowl.

## GUMMY ORANGE PUNCH

1 gallon orange sherbet, softened

1 quart pineapple juice, chilled

1 liter lemon-lime soda, chilled

Gummi worms

**C**ombine sherbet and pineapple juice in a punch bowl; stir well. Add soda; stir until sherbet is almost dissolved. Decorate punch bowl with gummy worms. Serve immediately.

## PBJ SAND-WITCH

1 loaf white bread
your favorite peanut butter
your favorite jelly
ghost or witch cookie cutter

**M**ake sandwiches. Cut out shapes with cookie cutter. Serve on a Halloween platter or paper plates. Kids love to make these.

# CHRISTMAS

# NOTES:

## CANDY CANE CUPCAKES

**1 box of white cake mix**

**1 teaspoon peppermint extract**

**8 drops green food coloring**

**1 can of vanilla frosting**

**½ cup crushed candy canes or red hots**

Preheat oven to 350°. Prepare cake as instructed on box, adding peppermint extract and food coloring. Pour mixture into lined muffin cups. Bake for 20-25 minutes or until done. Frost each cupcake with icing and top with candy.

## SANTA'S STRAWBERRY POUND CAKE

**1 box yellow butter cake mix**

**1 small box strawberry gelatin**

**⅔ cup vegetable oil**

**4 eggs**

**1 Tablespoon sugar**

**1 teaspoon vanilla**

**½ cup frozen strawberries**

Preheat oven to 350°. Mix all ingredients until well blended. Pour into greased tube pan. Bake for 45 minutes, or until toothpick inserted into center comes out clean.

## YULETIDE LEMON POUND CAKE

**2 cups self-rising flour**

**1 ⅓ cups sugar**

**½ pound butter, melted**

**5 eggs**

**2 teaspoons lemon flavoring**

Preheat oven to 350°. Mix all ingredients until well blended. Pour into greased tube pan. Bake for 30-40 minutes, or until toothpick inserted into center comes out clean

# HO HO CUPCAKES

**1 box cake mix (any flavor)**
**1 can vanilla frosting**
**chocolate chips**
**mini marshmallows**
**red sprinkles**

Preheat oven to 350°. Prepare cupcakes according to package directions, using paper cupcake holders. Cool. Frost with vanilla frosting.

To make Santa's face:

Sprinkle a line of red sprinkles across the top half of the cupcake (this will make the line for Santa's hat). Place 4 or 5 marshmallows over the sprinkles to make the hat. Use chocolate chips for the eyes and nose. Use 7 or 8 marshmallows for the beard.

*This is easy and fun! Your kids will want to do this every Christmas!*

# REINDEER CUPS

**1 box chocolate cake mix**
**Chocolate frosting**
**Chocolate sprinkles**
**Pecan halves**
**Pretzel sticks**
**Red gumdrops**
**Mini marshmallows**

Mix cake according to package directions. Pour batter into cupcake tins. Bake according to package directions and cool completely. Frost cupcakes so they are rounded on top. Sprinkle chocolate sprinkles on top. Insert 2 pecan halves to form ears and pretzels to form antlers. Use a gumdrop for the nose and cut marshmallows in half for the eyes.

## CHRISTMAS CUPCAKE CONES

Ice cream cones (flat on the
   bottom)
1 box any flavor cake mix
1 can icing (any flavor)
Shredded coconut
Chopped walnuts

Preheat oven to 350°. Place ice cream cones on a baking sheet. Prepare cake mix according to package directions. Pour cake batter into cones, leaving an inch of space at the top. Bake cupcake cones for 20-25 minutes. Remove from oven and let cool. Top with your favorite icing, adding coconut and walnuts. Add a drop of food coloring (red or green) to the coconut to make the cones more festive.

## SANTA CLAUS CAKE

1 cake mix (any flavor)
1 can pink frosting*
Mini marshmallows
Red gumdrops
Red string licorice
*or use white frosting and put a
   few drops of food coloring in
   the can to make it pink

Preheat oven to 350°. Spray the bottom of a 13 x 9 inch pan with non-stick vegetable spray. Mix cake according to package directions. Cool completely. Use licorice for hat. Shape licorice thinly at the top and thick at the end. Use marshmallows for tassel and brim of hat. Use marshmallow for beard and gumdrops for eyes and nose.

## PEANUT CHRISTMAS CRUNCH

6 cups Cap'n Crunch cereal,
   peanut butter flavor
1 can Spanish peanuts
1 lb. white almond bark
¼ cup smooth peanut butter

Combine cereal and peanuts and set aside. Combine almond bark and peanut butter in top of double boiler and cook until melted. Pour melted mixture over the tope of cereal/peanuts and stir with wooden spoon until coated. Drop by tablespoon onto cookie sheet. Place in refrigerator to cool. Store in airtight container.

# MOM'S FAVORITE FUDGE

### A quick, tasty treat for kids of all ages

- 3 cups sugar
- 1/3 cup cocoa
- 1 ½ cups milk
- 1 tablespoon butter
- 1 teaspoon vanilla
- ½ cup chopped pecans or walnuts, (optional)

In a heavy pan, bring sugar, cocoa and milk to a rolling boil. Boil until candy dropped in a cup of cold water forms soft ball. Remove from heat. Add butter and vanilla. Add nuts, if desired. Beat until candy begins to get hard. Pour into a buttered glass 8 x 8 inch dish. Cool and serve.

# JINGLE BELL BALLS

- 1 box powdered sugar
- 1 stick butter
- 2 cups peanut butter
- Chocolate bark (available in craft and grocery stores)

Mix first three ingredients and shape into balls. Chill. Melt bark. Drop chilled balls into chocolate mixture. Place on wax paper to harden. Store in a tight container.

# CANDY CANE COOKIES

- 1 (18-ounce) package refrigerated sugar cookie dough
- Flour
- 1 (12-ounce) package white chocolate morsels
- ½ cup crushed candy canes
- ¼ cup chopped walnuts or pecans

Preheat oven to 350°. Form dough into a ball and place on pizza pan or baking stone. Flatten slightly with the palm of your hand. Lightly flour dough and rolling pin. Roll dough into a 14-inch wide circle. Bake 18-20 minutes or until light golden brown. Remove dough from oven and immediately sprinkle morsels evenly over cookie. Let stand 2 to 3 minutes. Sprinkle with candy canes and nuts. Carefully loosen cookie from pan. Cool 5 minutes. Cut with pizza cutter. Makes 16 servings.

Aa Bb Cc Dd Ee Ff Gg Hh Ii Jj Kk Ll Mm Nn Oo Pp

## SNOWBALL COOKIES

- 1 (14-ounce) package flaked coconut
- 1 teaspoon almond extract
- 1 ½ cups M&M, plain or peanut chocolate candies
- 1 (14-ounce) can sweetened condensed milk
- ¼ teaspoon salt

Preheat oven to 350°. Combine all ingredients. Mix well. Drop by rounded Tablespoonfuls onto greased cookie sheet. Bake at 350° for 10-12 minutes or until they are lightly browned. Cool thoroughly on wire rack. Makes 3 dozen.

## ELVES EASY COOKIES

- 1 box white cake mix
- 2 packages chocolate pudding
- ½ to ¾ cup chopped nuts
- 12-ounce package of chocolate chips

Preheat oven to 350°. Mix all ingredients. Form into balls and place on greased cookie sheet. Bake until done.

## MRS. CLAUS GINGERSNAPS

- 1 teaspoon sugar
- ¾ cup shortening
- ¼ cup molasses
- 1 egg
- 1 teaspoon ginger
- 1 teaspoon ground cloves
- 1 teaspoon cinnamon
- 2 teaspoons baking soda
- 2 cups flour
- 1 cup granulated sugar (set aside)

Preheat oven to 350°. Cream 1 teaspoon sugar with shortening; add molasses and egg. Beat well. Add rest of ingredients (except 1 cup sugar). Roll into balls, then roll in granulated sugar. Place on greased cookie sheet. Bake at 350° for 8-10 minutes or until done.

## CHRISTMAS MORNING COOKIES

2 egg whites

²/₃ cup sugar

pinch of salt

1 teaspoon vanilla

1 cup chopped nuts

1 cup chocolate chips

Preheat oven to 350°. Beat egg whites until stiff. Fold in remaining ingredients. Spoon onto well greased or foil lined cookie sheet. Place in preheated oven and immediately turn off heat. Let cookies remain in oven overnight. Do not open the door until the next morning.

## COMET AND CUPID'S CRUNCHY BARS

1 12-ounce package semi-sweet chocolate morsels

1 can sweetened condensed milk

1 package chocolate wafers, crushed

1 cup chopped nuts, divided

Melt chocolate morsels in top of double boiler, stirring occasionally. Add condensed milk, chocolate wafers and ½ of the nuts. Stir until all are blended. Pour into 9 × 9 square pan. Press ½ the nuts on top. Cool and cut into squares.

## SHEPHERDS SURPRISE SQUARES

1 cup crunchy peanut butter

½ cup sugar

½ cup corn syrup

3 cups cornflakes

6-ounces chocolate chips

In saucepan, heat peanut butter, sugar and corn syrup, over low heat. Fold in cereal. Press mixture into 9-inch square pan that has been sprayed with non-stick coating. Melt chocolate and spread over top. Cool and cut into squares.

Aa Bb Cc Dd Ee Ff Gg Hh Ii Jj Kk Ll Mm Nn Oo Pp

## SANTA'S SUGAR COOKIES

½ cup sugar
½ cup brown sugar
1 cup shortening
1 egg
1 teaspoon vanilla
2 cups self-rising flour
Green and red sprinkles

Preheat oven to 350°. Cream sugars, shortening, egg and vanilla. Add flour. Dough will be stiff. Form into balls and place on ungreased cookie sheet. Dip fork in cold water and press each cookie. Sprinkle with red and green sprinkles. Bake at 350° for 8-10 minutes.

## NUTTY COCONUT COOKIE BARS

½ cup butter
1 ½ cups graham cracker crumbs
1 14.5-ounce can Eagle brand milk
6-ounce package chocolate chips
1 ⅓ cups coconut
1 cup chopped nuts

Preheat oven to 350°. Melt butter in a 13 x 9 inch baking pan. Sprinkle crumbs over butter; pour Eagle brand over crumbs; top with remaining ingredients. Press gently to flatten. Bake 20-30 minutes at 350°, or until lightly brown. Cool before cutting.

## FRUITY CHRISTMAS WREATHS

This is an easy variation of rice cereal treats!

2 tablespoons butter
2 ⅔ cups marshmallows
4 ½ cups fruity cereal

Melt butter in large saucepan. Add marshmallows and stir until melted. Add cereal to melted marshmallow mixture. Mix with wooden spoon until well coated. Grease your hands and shape the mixture into wreath shapes. Cool on waxed paper.

Children love this one.

Qq  Rr  Ss  Tt  Uu  Vv  Ww  Xx  Yy  Zz  1 2 3 4 5 6 7 8 9 10

## MERRY CHERRY COOKIES

**2 cups graham crackers**

**1 cup nuts**

**½ cup red candied cherries**

**1 cup coconut**

**1 stick butter**

**2 cups sugar**

**½ cup evaporated milk**

**2 cups mini marshmallows**

Break graham crackers into bite size pieces. Chop nuts and cherries. Add to graham crackers. Add coconut and set aside. Combine butter, sugar and evaporated milk in saucepan. Bring to a boil and boil for 4-5 minutes, stirring constantly. Remove from heat and add marshmallows and continue to stir until marshmallows are melted. Combine with graham cracker mixture, stirring well. Drop by teaspoons onto wax paper and chill. Store in airtight container.

## MERRY GRAHAM TREATS

**1 package graham crackers**

**¾ cup butter**

**½ cup sugar**

**1 cup chopped pecans or walnuts**

Separate each graham cracker into four sections. Line bottom of pan with tin foil. Melt butter in pan, stirring in sugar and pecans. Bring mixture to a boil for 3 minutes, stirring frequently. Spread mixture evenly over crackers. Bake for 12 minutes. Remove from pan and let cool on wax paper.

## SNOW LOGS

**1 banana**

**Peanut butter**

**Shredded coconut**

Cut banana into three pieces. Coat each piece with peanut butter. Roll pieces in coconut.

Aa Bb Cc Dd Ee Ff Gg Hh Ii Jj Kk Ll Mm Nn Oo Pp

## SANTA'S REINDEER

¼ cup peanut butter, creamy
2 slices of whole wheat bread
16 raisins
4 cherries
16 pretzels (twist type)

Spread peanut butter on bread and slice into four triangles. Turn triangles so the point is down. Place two raisins in the center of each triangle for eyes, cut cherry in half and place half at the bottom of the point for the nose. Break twist pretzels to make antlers and place at upper two corners.

## MRS. CLAUS' FAMOUS CHOCOLATE DIPPED PUFFS

3 cups puffed cereal
1 box confectioners sugar
2 cups chunky peanut butter
1 stick butter
16-ounces chocolate chips

Mix cereal and sugar until well blended. Add peanut butter and butter to cereal mixture and mix well. Place in refrigerator. Melt chocolate. Remove chilled mixture from the refrigerator and shape into balls. Dip into chocolate and place on waxed paper to harden.

## CHRISTMAS WREATHS

½ cup butter
35 large marshmallows
1 teaspoon vanilla
1 ½ teaspoons green food coloring
5 cups corn flakes
Red hots or cherries

Melt butter with marshmallows. Add vanilla and food coloring. Pour over corn flakes and mix until well coated. Drop by teaspoon onto waxed paper. Put "red hots" or cherry halves in the middle to form a wreath. Chill about 40 minutes. Makes 2 dozen.

## FROSTY'S FROZEN KOOL AID PIE

**1 large can Pet Milk, chilled**

**1 cup sugar**

**1 package any flavor Kool Aid**

**1 vanilla wafer crust (can be purchased already made)**

Whip milk; add sugar and then Kool Aid. Beat until thick. Pour into vanilla wafer crust. Chill.

*This is really good when it's frozen.*

## REINDEER PUFFS

**1 ½ cups chocolate chips**

**½ cup chunky peanut butter**

**2 tablespoons butter**

**36 or more large marshmallows**

**½ cup chopped pecans**

In the top of a double boiler, combine first three ingredients. Heat, stirring occasionally until melted. Place marshmallows in 9 x 9 inch square pan and pour the chocolate mixture over them. Sprinkle pecans on top. Chill until firm and cut into squares.

## KRIS KRINGLES CARAMEL CORN

**1 pound brown sugar**

**½ cup white corn syrup**

**1 cup butter**

**½ teaspoon baking soda**

**20 cups popped corn**

Preheat oven to 250°. Boil first three ingredients for 4 minutes. Remove from heat and stir in baking soda. Pour over popped corn and bake in large roasting pan in low oven for 1 hour. Stir every 15 minutes. Remove from oven, spread to cool. Break apart.

# LINDA'S FAKE FRUIT CAKE

*You don't bake this and it's so tasty
even your kids will eat it!*

- **1 pound pecans, chopped**
- **1 pound walnuts, chopped**
- **1 box of seedless raisins**
- **1 big box of vanilla wafers, crushed**
- **1 can 14.5-ounce Eagle brand milk**

**M**ix all ingredients and pack into a loaf pan. Chill for 24 hours.

# RUDOLPH'S BED TIME SNACK

- **3 ½ teaspoons peanut butter**
- **1 6-ounce package butterscotch morsels**
- **3 cups corn flakes**
- **½ cup nuts**

**M**elt peanut butter. Remove from heat and add butterscotch chips, corn flakes and nuts. Mix until blended. Drop by teaspoons onto waxed paper.

# LANE'S BUNCO CHRISTMAS SLUSHY

*My friend is famous for this punch recipe.
She always has a gallon on hand for wedding or baby showers,
and especially bunco parties.*

- **2 small packages strawberry Kool Aid**
- **1 large package cherry Kool Aid (with sugar)**
- **1 ½ cups sugar**
- **1 can unsweetened pineapple juice**

**M**ix all ingredients in 1 gallon container. If necessary, finish filling with water. Freeze. Set out 2 hours before serving.

## FA LA LA LA PUNCH

2 liters ginger ale
2 liters 7-up
½ gallon sherbert

**P**our ginger ale and 7-up into punch bowl. Add sherbet. Use the flavor sherbet needed for desired color of punch.

## GRANNY'S CHOCOLATE GRAVY

2 teaspoon butter
1 cup sugar
2 tablespoons cocoa
2 tablespoons flour
2 cups water

**M**ix all ingredients in sauce pan. Boil until thick. Pour over hot biscuits for a sweet, Christmas morning treat!

## HOT CHRISTMAS CIDER

1 gallon apple cider
2 sticks cinnamon
1 teaspoon whole cloves

**H**eat all ingredients, but do not boil.

Aa Bb Cc Dd Ee Ff Gg Hh Ii Jj Kk Ll Mm Nn Oo P

# VALENTINE

# NOTES:

### Author's Notes

Valentine's Day is such a great holiday. I have discovered that it's not just for me and my husband, but for everyone that I love. I have used several of these recipes at this time of year as gifts. Take a few precious minutes and make a list of those people who are dear to you, because they help you in so many ways. That special friend who picks your child up at dance class when you're running late, or the one who takes your child to ball practice when you just can't make it. Friends are so important to us, and sometimes we forget how much they really do mean to us. Let them know that you do appreciate them by giving them a sweet tasting gift.

## CRAZY ABOUT YOU DROPS

**2 cups almonds**

**2 egg whites**

**1 cup brown sugar**

**2 tablespoons sifted flour**

Preheat oven to 325°. Spray cookie sheet with non-stick spray or line with foil. Chop almonds into small pieces and set aside. Beat egg whites until stiff. Fold in brown sugar, flour and almonds. Carefully mix until well blended. Drop by teaspoons onto cookie sheet. Bake 10-12 minutes. Cool and serve.

## HONEY BARS

**½ cup sugar**

**½ cup honey**

**½ cup peanut butter**

**3 cups Cheerios**

**1 cup peanuts**

Mix sugar and honey and bring to a boil. Remove from heat. Stir in peanut butter until all is blended. Add Cheerios and peanuts and mix until well coated. Spread in a buttered 13 x 9-inch pan. Cool and cut into squares.

## CUPID'S CUPS

**Valentine cup cake liners**

**1 box chocolate cake mix**

**2 eggs**

**⅓ cup water**

**¼ cup oil**

**24 mini-peanut butter cup candies**

Preheat oven to 350°. Place cupcake liners in muffin pan. Prepare cupcakes according to package directions, except bake the cupcakes for 10 minutes and then remove from the oven. Place 1 peanut butter cup candy in the center of each cupcake, return to oven and bake for another 10 minutes. Cool and serve.

## VALENTINE THUMBPRINT COOKIES

**1 (8-ounce) package cream cheese, softened**

**1 stick butter, softened**

**1 cup flour**

**Strawberry Jam**

**Confectioner's sugar**

Whip together cream cheese and butter. Add flour and mix until well blended. Roll dough into a log and wrap in waxed paper. Chill until firm. Slice dough into ¼-inch slices. Place a thumbprint in the middle of each cookie and place ½ teaspoon strawberry jam in the center of each thumbprint. Bake until brown in a 350° oven (about 10 minutes). Cool and sprinkle with confectioner's sugar.

### Valentine Gift Ideas

 Wrap cookies in colorful (red) plastic wrap and tie with a white ribbon. Use cookies instead of Valentine cards for your child's class party. Be sure to include a small card with each cookie wrap with your child's name printed on it.

## LOVE BUG COOKIES

1 stick butter

2 cups sugar

2 tablespoons cocoa

½ cup milk

½ cup peanut butter

3 cups oats

1 teaspoon vanilla

Mix butter, sugar, cocoa and milk in a large saucepan, bring to a boil for one minute. Add peanut butter, oats and vanilla. Butterscotch bits may be added at this point, if desired. Mix well and drop by teaspoonful onto waxed paper.

## VALENTINE FRUIT PUNCH

1 package orange-cherry Kool Aid

1 package lemon-strawberry Kool Aid

2 cups sugar

1 quart water

1 6-ounce can frozen orange juice (undiluted)

1 6-ounce can frozen lemonade concentrate (undiluted)

1 quart ginger ale

Mix Kool Aid, sugar and water. Add orange juice and lemonade concentrate. Mix until frozen concentrates are thawed. Add ginger ale just before serving.

## HEART WARMING FUDGE

2 cups sugar

1 tablespoon cocoa

1 cup milk

1 tablespoon butter

1 teaspoon vanilla

Cook sugar, cocoa and milk over medium heat stirring constantly. Bring mixture to a boil, and as candy starts to thicken, remove from heat and add vanilla and butter. Beat mixture until firm. Pour into a buttered pan. Cool and cut into squares.

Qq Rr Ss Tt Uu Vv Ww Xx Yy Zz 1 2 3 4 5 6 7 8 9 10

## VALENTINE PIECES

**1 pound red candy coating**

**3 cups puffed rice cereal**

**M**elt candy coating on low heat. Do not over boil. Stir in cereal until well coated. Spread mixture on a wax paper lined cookie sheet. Cool until firm. Break into pieces. Can be stored in an air tight container.

## DREAMY DELIGHTS

**1 cup butter**

**¾ cup brown sugar**

**1 ½ cups pecan pieces (divided)**

**1 teaspoon vanilla extract**

**2 ½ cups flour**

**½ teaspoon baking powder**

**1 cup semi-sweet chocolate chips**

**P**reheat oven to 350°. Melt butter. In large bowl, mix butter, brown sugar, ¾ cup chopped pecan pieces and vanilla extract until well blended. Add flour and baking powder, mixing well. Shape dough into 1-inch balls. Place on ungreased cookie sheet. Bake 10-12 minutes in a 350° oven. Remove from heat and cool completely. On low heat, melt chocolate chips, stirring constantly until smooth. Dip cookies in melted chocolate, then roll in remaining pecan pieces. Cool until chocolate sets.

What did the boy octopus say
to the girl octopus on Valentines Day?

I want you hold your hand, hand,

Aa Bb Cc Dd Ee Ff Gg Hh Ii Jj Kk Ll Mm Nn Oo Pp

## CHERRY CHOCOLATE SURPRISE CUPCAKES

- **1 box chocolate cake mix**
- **1 can ready to spread chocolate frosting**
- **1 cup chocolate ice cream topping**
- **Maraschino cherries (drained)**
- **Whipped topping**

**P**reheat oven to 350°. Prepare cupcakes per package directions. Cool. Frost cupcakes. Put 1 teaspoon ice cream topping, 1 teaspoon whipped topping and a cherry on top of each cupcake.

## PEPPERMINT CRACKERS

- **1 pound chocolate bark**
- **1 box round butter crackers**
- **4-5 drops peppermint flavoring**

**M**elt chocolate in top of a double boiler or over very low heat in a regular saucepan. After chocolate is melted, stir in drops of peppermint flavor. Dip crackers into mixture and set on waxed paper until set.

## BE MINE ANGEL FOOD CAKE

- **1 large angel food cake**
- **1 carton whipped topping**
- **2 tablespoons sugar**
- **1 8-ounce package cream cheese**
- **1 can strawberry pie filling**

**S**lice cake in half (through the middle). Mix whipped topping, 2 tablespoons sugar, and cream cheese until well blended. Spread in a 1-½ inch layer on bottom half of the cake. Top with the other half of the cake. Ice with remaining cream cheese icing and top with strawberry pie filling.

---

## EASY SNICKERS FUDGE

**1 (12-ounce) package semi-sweet chocolate chips**

**2 (3.7 ounce) Snickers candy bars, chopped, divided**

**1 (15.6 ounce) can creamy milk chocolate frosting**

Line an 8-inch square pan with foil, extending over edges. Lightly spray pan with non-stick cooking spray. Set aside. Melt chips in medium saucepan over low heat, stirring constantly, then remove from heat. Reserve 2 tablespoons of Snickers. Add remaining Snickers and frosting to chocolate chips and blend well. Spread mixture on foil-lined pan. Crush remaining candy bars and sprinkle on top. Refrigerate 1 hour until firm.

---

## CHOCOLATE ÉCLAIR CAKE

**1 large box vanilla pudding mix**

**1 8-ounce container whipped topping**

**1 package graham crackers**

**1 can ready to spread chocolate icing**

Combine dry pudding mix and whipped topping. In a long cake pan, place a layer of graham crackers, then a layer of pudding mix and a second layer of crackers, a second layer of pudding mix and a third layer of crackers. Top with icing. Chill in refrigerator overnight. Cut into squares. This is a great dessert to take to work the next morning.

What is the difference between a girl who is sick
of her boyfriend and a sailor who falls into the ocean?

One is bored over a man and
the other is a man overboard.

---

Aa Bb Cc Dd Ee Ff Gg Hh Ii Jj Kk Ll Mm Nn Oo Pp

## SWEETIE PIE

1 8-ounce package cream cheese, softened

1 cup sugar

1 teaspoon vanilla extract

2/3 cup peanut butter

1 small container of whipped topping

1 ready made chocolate pie crust

Beat cream cheese, sugar and vanilla together. Add peanut butter and mix until well blended. Fold in whipped topping. Pour into chocolate pie crust. Freeze or cool and serve. You can also add chocolate sprinkles to the top right before serving.

## BUTTERFINGER DREAMS

¾ cup sugar

1/3 cup butter

1 egg

1 1/3 cups sifted flour

½ teaspoon baking soda

¼ teaspoon salt

¾ cup chopped butterfinger candy bars

Preheat oven to 350°. Spray the bottom of a cookie sheet with non-stick coating. Cream butter and sugar until fluffy. Beat in egg. In a separate bowl, mix flour, soda and salt together. Add candy pieces to dry mixture. Stir the butter mixture and the flour mixture together until well blended. Drop by teaspoons on cookie sheet. Bake for 8-10 minutes. Cool and serve.

## PEANUT DROPS

1 large box chocolate pudding

½ cup evaporated milk

1 cup sugar

1 tablespoon butter

1 cup salted peanuts

Mix first four ingredients in a large saucepan and bring to a boil. Boil for three to four minutes. Remove from heat. Add peanuts and stir until mixture begins to thicken. Drop by rounded teaspoons onto waxed paper. Cool before serving.

## VALENTINE POPCORN BALLS

1 cup light corn syrup

½ cup sugar

1 package red gelatin

10 cups popped popcorn

**M**ix syrup and sugar in a medium saucepan and bring to a boil. Remove from heat. Add gelatin and stir until blended. Pour mixture over popped corn and mix until well coated. Shape into balls and serve.

## SARA BETH'S STRAWBERRY DELIGHT

4 cups strawberries, sliced

1 jar strawberry glaze

8-10 Twinkies

1 8-ounce package cream cheese, softened

1 14-½ ounce can sweetened, condensed milk

1 large container whipped topping

**M**ix strawberries and glaze until well blended. Set aside. Slice Twinkies in half (lengthwise) and place a single layer in a 13 x 9-inch pan. Beat cream cheese and milk until smooth. Fold in whipped topping. Spread mixture over Twinkies. Spoon strawberry mixture over top. Chill and serve.

## SIMPLE COOKIES

1 box butter flavored cake mix

½ cup vegetable oil

2 eggs

2 tablespoons water

1 cup M&M baking chips or peanut butter chips (pick one)

**P**reheat oven to 350°. Mix first four ingredients. Then fold in baking chips or peanut butter chips. Drop by teaspoonful onto a coated cookie sheet. Bake in a 350°oven until lightly brown. Do not overbake. This is so simple, it's a great way to teach kids to bake.

Aa Bb Cc Dd Ee Ff Gg Hh Ii Jj Kk Ll Mm Nn Oo Pp

## LIP SMACKIN' CARAMEL DROPS

**50-60 caramels**

**2 tablespoons water**

**2 tablespoons butter**

**3 cups pecan pieces**

**10 ounces semi-sweet chocolate chips**

**3 ounces paraffin**

Melt caramels, water and butter in the top of a double boiler, or over low heat in a medium saucepan. Add pecan pieces. Mix until well blended. Drop by teaspoons onto a wax paper lined cookie sheet. Cool and let set. Melt chocolate chips and paraffin together. Dip caramel drops into chocolate mixture. Return drops to cookie sheet and let cool. Serve. May be stored in an air tight container.

## BE MY BABY BUTTERSCOTCH BARS

**1 ¼ cup shortening**

**1 cup brown sugar**

**1 egg**

**1 teaspoon vanilla**

**⅔ cup all purpose flour**

**1 teaspoon baking powder**

**½ cup walnut pieces**

**¼ teaspoon salt**

Preheat oven to 350°. Spray the bottom of a 9-inch square pan with non-stick vegetable spray. Cream shortening, brown sugar, vanilla and eggs. Mix until well blended. In another bowl, mix flour, baking powder, walnuts, and salt. Add flour mixture to egg mixture. Stir until well blended. Spread mixture into a 9-inch pan. Bake in a 350° oven for 20-25 minutes. Cool and cut into bars.

What did the Valentine card say to the stamp?

Stick with me and we'll go places.

## COCONUT KISSES

2 (1 ounce) squares
   unsweetened chocolate

1 (14 ounce) can sweetened
   condensed milk

3 cups flaked coconut

1 teaspoon vanilla

dash of salt

whole almonds

**P**reheat oven to 350°. Spray a cookie sheet with non-stick vegetable spray or line the cookie sheet with aluminum foil. Heat chocolate and milk over low heat, stirring frequently to avoid scorching the milk. Add coconut, vanilla and salt. Stir until coconut is well coated. Drop by teaspoons onto cookie sheet. Place an almond in the center of each coconut ball. Bake in a 350° oven for 8-12 minutes. Cool and serve.

## DELICIOUS DELIGHT

Not just for the kids! This is a great dessert to prepare the night before and take to the office for a special treat.

9-inch graham cracker crust

2 bananas, sliced

1 quart strawberry ice cream,
   softened

1 can crushed pineapple,
   drained

whipped topping

¼ cup walnut pieces

Maraschino cherries, drained

**P**lace bananas on bottom of graham cracker crust. Evenly spread ice cream over bananas. Spread pineapple over ice cream, then spread whipped topping. Sprinkle walnut pieces over whipped topping and top with cherries. This should be served immediately, or you can keep it overnight in the freezer and serve the next day. It tastes great frozen!

Patty's purple passion Percy
Passed his plate for pudding, please.
Patty paused and paled politely,
Passing Percy pureed peas.

Aa Bb Cc Dd Ee Ff Gg Hh Ii Jj Kk Ll Mm Nn Oo Pp

## BE MINE BUTTERFINGER PIE

**1 large box of chocolate pudding**

**1 large container of whipped topping**

**3 Butterfinger candy bars, cut into bite sized pieces**

**1 ready made chocolate pie crust**

**M**ix pudding according to package directions. Add whipped topping and candy pieces. Mix until all ingredients are well blended. Pour into pie crust. Chill and serve.

## PALS FOREVER PEANUT BUTTER PIE

**1 large box chocolate pudding mix**

**1/3 cup peanut butter**

**1 large carton whipped topping**

**1 ready made graham cracker crust**

**P**repare pudding according to package directions. Add peanut butter and mix until well blended. Add whipped topping. Mix well. Pour into graham cracker crust. Chill and serve.

## CUPID'S FAMOUS CARAMEL PIE

**3 tablespoons butter**

**4 tablespoons all purpose flour**

**1 cup sugar**

**1 egg**

**1 cup milk**

**1 teaspoon vanilla extract**

**1 ready made pie crust**

**whipped topping**

**C**ream butter, flour and sugar in a medium bowl. Set aside. In another bowl, beat egg and milk. Pour into butter mixture. Pour mixture into a medium saucepan and cook and stir over medium head until mixture thickens. Remove from heat and let cool. Add vanilla. Pour into prepared crust. Top with whipped topping. Chill and serve.

Qq Rr Ss Tt Uu Vv Ww Xx Yy Zz 1 2 3 4 5 6 7 8 9 10

## CHOCOLATE COVERED PRETZELS

**1 tablespoon heavy cream**

**2 cups semi-sweet chocolate chips**

**1 pound bag of pretzels (any shape)**

**M**elt chocolate and cream in the top of a double boiler over low heat. Stirring constantly. While mixture is still very warm, quickly dip pretzels in chocolate mixture, one at a time to coat. Place pretzels on waxed paper to cool.

## LIP SMACKIN' BARS

**16 ounces white baking chocolate**

**2 cups Oreo cereal, crushed**

**S**lowly heat chocolate in the top of a double boiler, stirring occasionally. When chocolate has melted, add crushed cereal. Gently mix until cereal is well coated. Spread on waxed paper or aluminum foil lined cookie sheet. Chill until firm. Break into bite size pieces or cut into squares.

What travels around the world but stays in one corner?

A stamp.

What does an envelope say when you lick it?

Nothing. It shuts up.

Aa Bb Cc Dd Ee Ff Gg Hh Ii Jj Kk Ll Mm Nn Oo Pp

# EASTER

Why is the Easter bunny so lucky?

# NOTES:

Because he has 4 rabbit's feet.

## BRYER PATCH POUND CAKE

1 ready made pound cake
Strawberry pie filling
1 large carton whipped topping
1 cup shredded coconut
1 teaspoon green food coloring
1 cup jelly beans
Mini marshmallows

Tint coconut with food coloring and set aside. Slice pound cake and line the bottom of a 13 x 9-inch pan with slices. Pour pie filling over cake. Spread whipped topping on top of pie filling. In center of cake, place tinted coconut. Add jelly beans and marshmallows.

## PRETTY PASTEL CUPCAKES

1 box white cake mix
¼ cup sugar sweetened soft drink mix – any flavor
Sprinkles
Pastel frosting (or make your own by adding food coloring to white frosting)

Bake cupcakes according to package directions, adding drink mix to cake batter during mixing. Remove from oven. Frost with ready made frosting, topping with sprinkles.

## PEANUT BUTTER BARS

1 large package refrigerator peanut butter cookie dough
1 12-ounce package peanut butter chips

Preheat oven to 350°. Spread cookie dough on a 13 x 9 cookie sheet. Bake cookie dough until light brown. Remove from oven. Pour chips over top and return to oven until chips melt. Cool and cut into squares.

# EASY TWINKIE DESSERT

1 box twinkies (12)

3 small boxes frozen strawberries, thawed

2 small boxes vanilla instant pudding

2 ½ cups milk

1 (14.5-ounce) can Eagle brand sweetened condensed milk

6-ounces whipped topping

Split twinkies in half lengthwise and place in a large dish. Pour thawed strawberries over twinkies. Mix pudding and milk in a small bowl. Add Eagle brand milk. Add whipped topping. Mix well. Pour over mixture over strawberries. Chill and serve.

# JELLY BEAN BIRDS NEST CUPCAKES

Any flavor cake mix

Any flavor frosting mix, or can of prepared frosting

Coconut

Jelly beans, Easter colors are best

Prepare cupcakes, according to package directions. When cool, frost with white or chocolate frosting. Sprinkle coconut around the edge of each cupcake. Place colored jelly beans in the center of each cupcake, for eggs. Coconut can be lightly toasted, if you prefer a brown nest.

*Alternate:* Tint coconut with green food coloring, place around edge of cupcake, use pastel M&M's for eggs and you've got an Easter basket cupcake.

## NO BAKE ORANGE BALLS

**1 package vanilla wafers, finely crushed**

**¾ cup coconut**

**½ cup frozen orange juice, thawed and undiluted**

**¾ cup confectioner's sugar**

**M**ix wafer crumbs, coconut and confectioner's sugar. Add orange juice and mix well. Form into 1 inch balls. Roll balls in confectioner's sugar. Refrigerate and serve chilled.

## CREATIVE CHOCOLATE COOKIES

**1 box German chocolate cake mix**

**1 container chocolate yogurt**

**1 egg**

**1 can chocolate frosting, ready made**

**P**reheat oven to 350°. Mix cake mix, yogurt and egg until smooth. Drop by teaspoons on greased baking sheet. Bake in a 350° oven for 10-12 minutes. Cool and top with frosting.

## BIRDS NESTS

**1 10-ounce package peanut butter chips**

**1 tablespoon shortening**

**1 large can chow mein noodles**

**1 bag pastel colored M&M's**

**M**elt peanut butter chips and shortening in a medium saucepan, stirring until well blended. Pour noodles into peanut butter mixture and stir until coated. Drop by tablespoons onto waxed paper, leaving and indentation in the middle. Place M&M's in each nest for eggs. Cool and serve.

## THROW TOGETHER COOKIE SQUARES

**1 stick butter**

**1 ½ cups graham cracker crumbs**

**1 ½ cups semi-sweet chocolate chips**

**1 ½ cups pecan pieces**

**1 can (14.5-ounce) Eagle brand condensed milk**

Preheat oven to 300°. Melt butter in a 13 × 9-inch pan. Spread graham cracker crumbs over butter. Spread chips over graham crackers. Sprinkle pecan chips over chocolate. Pour milk over entire mixture. Bake in a 300° oven for 35 minutes. Cool and cut into squares.

## GREAT BROWNIES

**1 package brownie mix**

**½ cup brown sugar**

**½ cup pecans (chopped)**

**3 tablespoons butter**

Preheat oven to 350°. Prepare brownies according to package directions. Spread in a greased 13 × 9-inch baking pan. Mix brown sugar, pecans and butter in a small bowl until blended. Pour gently over brownie mixture. Bake in a 350° oven for 30 minutes. Cool and cut into squares.

## CRUNCHY TOPPED BROWNIES

**1 package fudge brownie mix**

**½ cup rice cereal**

**½ cup pecan pieces**

Prepare brownie mix according to package directions. Pour into a coated 13 × 9-inch pan. Pour cereal over mix. Top with pecan pieces. Bake according to package directions on brownie mix. Cool and cut into squares.

## ROCKY ROAD CHOCOLATE BARS

**1 12-ounce package chocolate chips**

**2 ¼ cups mini marshmallows**

**½ cup chopped pecans**

**M**elt chocolate over low heat or in top of double boiler. Stir in remaining ingredients. Pour into square pan. Cool and cut into squares.

## CHOCOLATE CHERRY CHUNKS

**1 12-ounce package semi-sweet chocolate chips**

**¾ cups candied cherries**

**1 cup almond pieces**

**M**elt chips until smooth. Add other ingredients, mixing well. Drop by teaspoons onto wax paper. Cool.

## HOPPIN' GOOD TREATS

**1 8-ounce package cream cheese, softened**

**½ cup peanut butter**

**1 6-ounce package semi-sweet chocolate chips**

**2 ¼ cups graham cracker crumbs**

**Confectioner's Sugar**

**M**ix cream cheese and peanut butter until blended. Stir in chocolate pieces. Add graham cracker crumbs. Mix well. Roll into 1-inch balls. Roll in confectioner's sugar. Chill.

## COCONUT DREAMS

**⅔ cup sweetened condensed milk**

**3 cups shredded coconut**

**1 teaspoon vanilla extract**

**P**reheat oven to 350°. Combine all ingredients, mixing well. Drop by teaspoons on a greased cookie sheet. Bake in a 350° oven for 8-10 minutes.

## PETER COTTONTAILS

Caramel candy (35-40 pieces)
1 ½ tablespoons butter
½ cup pecan pieces
1 cup vanilla morsels (melted)
¾ cup flaked coconut

**M**elt caramels and butter in a large saucepan. Add pecans and remove from heat. Drop by teaspoons onto wax paper. Spool melted morsels over caramel mixture and top with coconut. Cool on waxed paper.

## BOPPIN' BISCUITS

1 can refrigerated biscuits
1 8-ounce package cream cheese (softened)
coconut or cinnamon

**P**reheat oven according to package directions. Place biscuits on cookie sheet. Make an indentation in the center of each biscuit. Put tablespoon of cream cheese in the middle of each indentation, topping with coconut or cinnamon. Bake according to directions on package.

## COOL COCONUT PIE

1 9-inch prepared pie crust, any flavor
1 small box vanilla instant pudding
1 ½ cups milk
1 ½ cups flaked coconut
1 container whipped topping (small)

**M**ix pudding mix and milk in a large bowl, until the pudding mixture thickens. Fold in 1 cup of coconut and half the whipped topping into the pudding. Pour mixture into prepared pie crust. Spread the remainder of the whipped topping on top of the pie. Sprinkle with remainder of the coconut. Chill and serve.

Aa Bb Cc Dd Ee Ff Gg Hh Ii Jj Kk Ll Mm Nn Oo Pp

SUMMER

Aa Bb Cc Dd Ee Ff Gg Hh Ii Jj Kk Ll Mm Nn Oo Pp Qq Rr Ss Tt Uu Vv Ww Xx Yy Zz 1 2 3 4 5 6 7 8 9 10

# NOTES:

## CREAMY CHERRY PIE

1 cup cold milk

1 teaspoon vanilla

2 packages whipped topping mix

¾ cup sugar

1 large package cream cheese, softened

1 (9-inch) graham cracker crust

1 (15-ounce) can cherry pie filling

**M**ix milk, vanilla and whipped topping together. Add sugar and cream cheese and beat well. Pour into graham cracker crust and top with cherry pie filling. Chill before serving.

## NO BAKE LEMONADE PIE

1 can frozen pink lemonade concentrate (thawed)

1 carton whipped topping

1 graham cracker crust

**M**ix lemonade and whipped topping until blended. Pour into pie crust. Cool and serve.

## CREAMY ORANGE JUICE PIE

1 (14.5 ounce) can Eagle brand condensed milk

1 small can frozen orange juice, thawed

1 large carton whipped topping

½ cup chopped pecans

2 graham cracker crusts

**M**ix all ingredients until well blended. Pour into pie crusts and chill until firm. This makes two pies.

## LEMON PIE

**3 egg yolks**

**7 tablespoons lemon juice**

**1 (14.5 ounce) can Eagle brand condensed milk**

**1 large carton whipped topping**

**1 large graham cracker crust**

**M**ix lemon juice and egg yolks. Fold in condensed milk and whipped topping. Stir until firm. Pour into pie crust. Chill until firm. Serve cold.

## SUNNY ORANGE PIE

**1 (4-serving size) package orange flavored gelatin**

**1 cup boiling water**

**1 pint vanilla ice cream, softened**

**1 prepared chocolate crumb pie crust**

**Whipped topping**

**D**issolve gelatin in boiling water. Spoon in ice cream, stirring until melted and smooth. Chill until slightly thickened, about 10 minutes. Pour gelatin mixture into pie crust. Chill until firm. Top with whipped topping. Can also add chocolate sprinkles to top of pie before chilling.

## PEANUT BRITTLE PIE

**1 package whipped topping**

**Milk**

**Vanilla**

**1 box peanut brittle, finely crushed**

**1 graham cracker crust**

**P**repare whipped topping, using milk and vanilla according to package directions. Add peanut brittle, mix and pour into pie crust. Chill. Serve shortly after it has been chilled.

Aa Bb Cc Dd Ee Ff Gg Hh Ii Jj Kk Ll Mm Nn Oo P

## NO BAKE CHEESECAKE PIE

1 can sweetened condensed milk

1 (8 ounce) package cream cheese, softened

1 teaspoon vanilla extract

¼ cup lemon juice

1 graham cracker crust

**B**lend milk and cream cheese. Stir in vanilla. Add lemon juice, blending all ingredients until mixed well. Pour into graham cracker crust. Chill and serve.

## POOL PARTY PIE

1 ½ cups cold milk

1 (4-serving size) package instant vanilla pudding

3 ½ cups whipped topping

1 cup chocolate sandwich cookies, chopped

1 prepared chocolate pie crust

**P**our cold milk into large bowl. Add pudding mix. Beat until well blended. Let stand until slightly thickened. Fold whipped topping and sandwich cookies into pudding mixture. Spoon into crust. Freeze overnight. Remove from freezer about 10 minutes before serving.

## DISAPPEARING ICE CREAM SANDWICHES

12 ice cream sandwiches

1 (8 ounce) carton whipped topping

2 large Butterfinger candy bars, crushed

**L**ine the bottom of a 13 x 9-inch glass dish with ice cream sandwiches. Spread whipped topping over sandwiches. Sprinkle Butterfinger crumbs over the top. Cover and freeze until ready to serve. Makes 8.

Can also substitute crushed peanut brittle or Nestle crunch bars.

## CHOCOLATE ICE CREAM

**2 cans Eagle brand condensed milk**

**12 ounces frozen whipped topping**

**½ gallon chocolate milk**

**¾ cup chocolate syrup**

**M**ix all ingredients and freeze. Serve chilled

## SURPRISE SURPRISE

**1 6 ounce package strawberry gelatin**

**1 pint vanilla ice cream**

**1 pint strawberry ice cream**

**marshmallows and sprinkles**

**M**ix gelatin according to package directions. Pour into a bundt cake pan and chill. When gelatin is firm, remove from pan by turning out onto a serving plate. Add ice cream to the middle of the mold. Top with marshmallows and sprinkles.

*You will be surprised at how good this is!*

## CHOCOLATE PEANUT BUTTER ICE CREAM

**12 ounces vanilla ice cream**

**¼ cup crunchy peanut butter**

**1 cup whipped topping**

**1 package (large) instant chocolate pudding**

**M**ix all ingredients. Pour into a square pan and freeze.

Aa Bb Cc Dd Ee Ff Gg Hh Ii Jj Kk Ll Mm Nn Oo Pp

## MILLION DOLLAR PIE

1 large carton whipped topping

1 can Eagle brand condensed milk

1 cup pecans, crushed

1 can pineapple (drained)

1/3 cup lemon juice

1 can coconut

2 graham cracker pie crusts

**M**ix all ingredients and pour into pie shells. Chill and serve. This will make two pies.

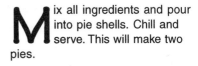

## FRUITY FROZEN DESSERT

1 large carton whipped topping

1 can strawberry pie filling

1 can crushed pineapple

½ cup pecan pieces

**M**ix all ingredients well and pour into bundt pan. Freeze. Turn onto a serving plate when frozen. This is very pretty and it tastes wonderful!

## ICE CREAM/BANANA BOATS

### A great sleep over treat!

½ gallon vanilla ice cream

½ gallon chocolate ice cream

½ gallon strawberry ice cream

6 bananas

1 jar caramel topping

1 jar strawberry topping

whipped topping

chopped nuts, if desiired

**P**lace one scoop of each flavor ice cream into a dish. Split banana lengthwise and place on the side of the ice cream. Spoon 1 tablespoon of each topping on ice cream. Top with whipped topping. Add nuts if desired.

Qq Rr Ss Tt Uu Vv Ww Xx Yy Zz 1 2 3 4 5 6 7 8 9 10

## SASSY STRAWBERRY SHORTCAKE

1 angel food cake

1 (6 ounce) package strawberry gelatin

2 (10 ounce) boxes frozen strawberries, thawed

1 (5 ¼ ounce) box vanilla instant pudding

whipped topping

Crumble cake into a large bowl. Set aside. Prepare strawberry jello per package instructions. Add thawed strawberries. Set aside. Prepare vanilla pudding per package directions. Pour strawberry mixture over cake, then add pudding. Do not mix. Refrigerate until set. Garnish with whipped topping.

## LEMONADE COOKIES

1 cup butter

1 cup sugar

2 eggs

3 cups sifted all purpose flour

1 teaspoon baking soda

1 can (6 ounce) lemonade concentrate, thawed

Preheat oven to 350°. Cream butter and sugar; add eggs. Set aside. Mix flour and baking soda together Add to butter/sugar mixture. Add lemonade and mix well. Drop by rounded tablespoons onto a greased cookie sheet. Bake in a 350° oven for 8-10 minutes until edges are brown. Sprinkle tops with sugar.

## BISCUITS GALORE

1 can buttermilk biscuits

bananas

honey

confectioner's sugar

Prepare biscuits according to package directions. Split biscuits in half. Pour 3-4 squeezes of honey on each half. Mash bananas in a bowl. Place mashed banana on each half of the biscuit. Put halves back together. Pour honey and confectioner's sugar on plate around biscuits.

## LET'S DO THE TWIST BISCUITS

**1 package refrigerator biscuits**
**½ cup melted butter**
**1 cup cinnamon and 1 cup sugar, mixed**

Preheat oven to 350°. Stretch biscuits into an oval shape. Dip into melted butter, coating both sides. Dip into cinnamon sugar mix, coating both sides. Twist biscuits about three or four times, twisting in one direction. Place on a cookie sheet. Bake in a 350° oven about 10 minutes, until brown. Do not overbake.

## TACO SHELL BREAKFAST

**1 taco shell**
**butter**
**cinnamon**
**sugar**

Spread butter all over the taco shell. Sprinkle the cinnamon and sugar over butter. Place in microwave for 20 seconds on high or until taco shell is warm.

This is a kid friendly food – they can make it themselves and it's a sweet breakfast treat.

## NUTTY CRACKERS

**Saltine crackers**
**1 (16-ounce) package chocolate chips**
**1 cup butter**
**1 cup brown sugar**
**1 cup chopped walnuts**

Preheat oven to 350°. Line a 13 x 9-inch baking pan with crackers. Melt butter; add brown sugar and stir until blended; pour over crackers. Place in a 350° oven for 10 minutes. Remove from oven and add chocolate chips on top. Sprinkle with nuts. Return to oven for 10 minutes, until chocolate melts. Remove from oven and cut into squares.

## PIGEON POOP

5 cups peanut butter
2 cups rice cereal
2 cups pretzel sticks
2 pounds of white chocolate
2 ½ cups mini marshmallows

Mix first three ingredients in a large bowl. Melt white chocolate over low heat. Pour over dry ingredients until coated. Spread on waxed paper until cool. Break into chunks.

## CLOBS

Chocolate chips
Graham crackers
Peanut butter

Melt chocolate chips and spread on graham crackers. Spread peanut butter on graham crackers. Put the crackers together like a sandwich. Freeze for about 30-45 minutes.

## SWEET TIME DESSERT

1 large package cherry gelatin
2 cups boiling water
1 can cherry pie filling
1 20 ounce can crushed
  pineapple, undrained
½ cup nuts
Whipped topping for garnish

Dissolve gelatin in boiling water; add remaining ingredients (except whipped topping). Cool and serve with whipped topping.

## CEREAL TREATS

¼ cup butter

⅓ cup grated parmesan cheese

3 cups Kix corn cereal

2 cups corn chips

**M**elt butter in large saucepan. Stir in cheese and stir until melted. Remove from heat. Add cereal and corn chips until well coated. Spread into a 9 × 9-inch square pan. Cool and cut into squares.

## CHOCOLATE PEANUT BUTTER BARS

1 tablespoon butter

½ cup light corn syrup

1 package semi-sweet chocolate chips

¼ cup peanut butter

1 ½ cups mini marshmallows

5 cups peanut butter puff cereal

**I**n a large saucepan, melt butter, corn syrup, marshmallows and chips over low heat. Add peanut butter and mix until smooth and well blended. Add cereal until coated. Remove from heat. Press mixture into a 9 × 9-inch square pan. Cool and cut into bars.

## CHOCOLATE PEANUTS

¼ cup white chocolate

¼ cup milk chocolate

½ cup peanuts

**M**elt chocolate in a small saucepan. Add peanuts. Mix until well coated. Drop by teaspoonful onto waxed paper. Cool.

Qq  Rr  Ss  Tt  Uu  Vv  Ww  Xx  Yy  Zz    1 2 3 4 5 6 7 8 9 10

## SO EASY STRAWBERRY CAKE

2 cans strawberry pie filling
1 box white cake mix
1 cup pecan pieces
2 sticks butter, melted

Preheat oven to 350°. Spread pie filling over bottom of 9 x 9-inch baking pan; sprinkle cake mix on top; sprinkle nuts on top of cake mix. Pour melted butter over all. Do not mix. Bake in a 350° oven for 35-40 minutes. Super, super easy! The kids can do this with just a little supervision.

## SUMMER FRUIT SALAD

1 can Eagle brand condensed milk
1 can cherry pie filling
1 can crushed pineapple
½ cup walnut pieces
8 ounces whipped topping

Mix first four ingredients in a large bowl. Chill. Serve with whipped topping.

## O'S BARS

2 tablespoons butter
1 bag mini marshmallows
5 cups cheerios

Melt butter and marshmallows in a large pan over low heat. Add cereal and mix until coated. Press into a 13 x 9-inch baking pan. Cool and serve.

## BACKYARD HOBO POPCORN

### This is a great treat for back yard camp outs!

You'll need a barbecue grill with a flame,
or a campfire for this one. Be sure that Dad or Mom
supervises this adventurous treat.

**1 18-inch square of heavy duty aluminum foil**

**4 teaspoons cooking oil**

**4 tablespoons popcorn**

**melted butter**

**salt**

Cut the 18-inch square of heavy duty foil into four squares. In the center of each square, place one teaspoon oil and 1 tablespoon popcorn. Bring the four corners of the foil to the center, making a pouch like a hobo's knapsack. Seal the edges so the popcorn doesn't escape while cooking. With a piece of wire, or string, tie the corners of each pouch to long handled barbecue tool or a green stick. Don't use a dry twig, or you'll catch the whole knapsack on fire!

Place pouch directly on hot coals and shake often until popcorn is popped. Open carefully and season popcorn with melted butter and salt.

Makes 4 servings.

## CRUNCHY BANANA BITS

**3 bananas**

**¼ cup milk**

**¼ cup honey**

**¼ cup granola**

**toothpicks**

Peel bananas and cut into bite sized pieces. Mix milk and honey and set aside. Put granola into a zip lock bag. Dip each banana piece into milk and honey mixture and drop into zip lock bag and shake until coated. Serve with toothpicks.

Qq  Rr  Ss  Tt  Uu  Vv  Ww  Xx  Yy  Zz  1 2 3 4 5 6 7 8 9 10

## ORANGE NUT BANANA SUPREMES

Bananas

½ cup orange juice

nuts or crushed cereal or
  granola

**C**ut bananas into bite size pieces. Dip into orange juice and roll in nuts or cereal.

## QUICK SUMMER PUNCH

1 quart grape juice, chilled

1 quart lemon lime soda,
  chilled

**C**ombine grape juice and lemon lime soda in a pitcher. Mix well.

## FROZEN SLURPIE

1 can frozen orange juice

2 cups Sprite or 7-Up

7 ounces pineapple juice

**M**ix all ingredients. Pour into plastic cups and serve after a ball game.

## BISCUITS OUTDOORS

Another back yard campout treat that will need supervision.

Biscuit mix

Milk or water

Honey

**P**repare biscuit mix according to package directions, using a little less liquid than called for in the instructions. Twist the dough around a clean coat hanger. Hold over a fire until brown. Dip in honey when complete. Can also top with butter.

Aa Bb Cc Dd Ee Ff Gg Hh Ii Jj Kk Ll Mm Nn Oo Pp

## SKILLET PIZZA SANDWICH

*This tastes best made in a cast iron skillet over an open flame.*
*You can make these in the kitchen,*
*if you don't have a campfire going.*

**Pizza sauce**
**Sliced bread**
**Mozzarella cheese**
**Pepperoni**
**Butter for cooking**

Spread pizza sauce on one slice of bread. Top with cheese and pepperoni. Top with another slice of bread. Melt butter in skillet, cook sandwich until cheese melts. Be sure to turn the sandwich over and cook both sides until bread is browned.

## GONE FISHIN'

**Celery sticks**
**Cheese spread**
**Goldfish crackers**

Trim and wash celery. Cut into logs. Fill each log with cheese spread. Top with crackers. A crunchy healthy treat!

## PEANUT BUTTER LOGS

**1 ¾ cups powdered sugar**
**¼ cup melted butter**
**1 cup chunky peanut butter**
**2 cups puffed rice cereal**
**1 can chocolate frosting**

Combine sugar and butter in a large bowl. Beat with electric mixer until smooth. Stir in peanut butter. Mix well with a spoon. Add cereal and mix again. Shape into logs. Spread tops with frosting. Ready to eat!

## SWEET BREAKFAST PIE

**2 slices of bread**
**pie filling (any flavor)**
**butter**

Place pie filling between two slices of bread. Close to make a sandwich. Melt butter in frying pan or spray with vegetable spray. Cook each side of sandwich until golden brown.

## GO BANANAS

**Bananas**
**Chocolate bars, broken**
**Mini marshmallows**
**Peanut butter**

Cut bananas lengthwise. Place bananas onto a square of heavy duty foil. Place broken candy bars and marshmallows and peanut butter on top of banana slices. Wrap in foil and place on campfire. All is done when marshmallows and chocolate are melted. Enjoy!

## S'MORE BALLS

**1 package graham cracker crumbs**
**1 can sweetened condensed milk**
**1 (12-ounce) package semi-sweet chocolate chips**
**½ cup nuts, chopped**
**1 package coconut**

Mix cracker crumbs, milk, chips and nuts together. Drop by rounded teaspoons into coconut. Roll in coconut and let stand on wax paper. Will be ready to pop into the kid's mouths in 10 minutes.

# JUST
# FOR MOM

# NOTES:

## BANANA BREAD

½ cup oil
¾ cup sugar
2 eggs, beaten
1 cup chopped pecans
3 ripe bananas
2 cups self-rising flour

Preheat oven to 350°. Mix all ingredients. Bake in a greased bread pan for 35-40 minutes.

## CHEESE BREAD

1 small package bisquick
1 cup cheddar cheese, grated
1 tablespoon solid shortening
½ cup plus 1 cup milk
1 egg, beaten

Preheat oven to 350°. Mix all ingredients. Bake in a greased bread pan for 30 minutes.

## EASY PEACH COBBLER

1 stick butter
1 cup sugar
1 cup flour
1 15-ounce can peaches
1 cup milk

Melt butter in baking dish. Mix sugar and flour together and pour on top of butter. Pour peaches on top of flour mixture. Bake for 30 minutes.

## MAYONNAISE ROLLS

2 tablespoons mayonnaise
1 cup self-rising flour
½ cup milk

Preheat oven to 425°. Mix all ingredients well. Spoon into greased muffin tins. Bake until brown.

# HERB BREAD

1 stick butter

1 tablespoon herb salad
dressing mix (dried)

1 loaf French or Italian bread

**M**elt butter and stir in 1-tablespoon herb salad dressing mix. Slice bread into thick slices, but do not cut through the bottom of the loaf. Brush each slice on both sides with butter/herb mixture, brushing remaining butter mix on top of load. Wrap bread in foil. Bake in 400° oven for 10-12 minutes. For crisper top, leave the foil wrap open, but watch bread so it does not burn.

# COCONUT CAKE

1 box yellow cake mix

1-½ cups milk

1-½ cups sugar

1 large carton of prepared
whipped topping

1 package coconut

**P**repare and bake cake as directed on package – bake in a 13 × 9-inch cake pan. Mix milks and sugar; bring to a complete boil. Boil for 1 minute. With a knife, punch holes in cake and pour milk/sugar mix over cake. Top cooled cake with whipped topping and coconut.

# DUMP CAKE

1 (20 ounce) can crushed
pineapple

1 can cherry pie filling

1 box yellow cake mix

1 cup chopped pecans

2 sticks butter

**P**reheat oven to 350°. Layer each of the first 4 ingredients in a 13 × 9 inch baking pan. Do not mix. Slice butter and drop on top of mixture. Bake for 1 hour in 350° oven.

Aa Bb Cc Dd Ee Ff Gg Hh Ii Jj Kk Ll Mm Nn Oo Pp

## NO BAKE BANANA PUDDING

1 package banana instant pudding

1 package vanilla wafers

1 carton prepared whipped topping

2 medium bananas

**P**repare pudding as directed on package. Add prepared whipped topping and sliced bananas. Mix wafers in with pudding or make alternate layers of wafers and pudding mix. Top with crumbled wafers.

## EASY BAKE CAKE

1 box yellow cake mix

1 can strawberry pie filling

1 can whipped cream

½ cup pecans, crushed

**M**ix cake and bake in 2 8-inch round cake pans, according to package directions. When cool, place each layer on an individual serving dish. Pour ½ can of strawberry pie filling in center of each cake. Frost each layer with whipped cream, leaving the strawberries showing in the middle. Sprinkle crushed pecans over each layer.

## POPCORN BUNDT CAKE

1 pound marshmallows

½ cup melted butter

½ cup corn oil

4 quarts popped corn, unsalted

½ pound gum drops

½ pound peanuts

**M**elt marshmallows, butter and corn oil in large saucepan. Mix popcorn, gum drops and peanuts in large bowl. Pour marshmallow mixture over popcorn mixture. Place mixture into a large bundt pan. Cool and serve.

## BEGINNER'S APPLE PIE

*A great way to introduce your children to the art of baking!*
*This is a can't miss recipe.*

**1 pie crust (2 piece), unbaked**

**1 can apple pie filling**

**1 stick butter**

**cinnamon**

**sugar**

Preheat oven to 350°. Place bottom piecrust into 9-inch pie plate. Pour apple pie filing into shell. Slice butter and place slices on top of pie filling. Sprinkle cinnamon and sugar (to taste) on top of butter. Place second pie crust on top of mixture, fluting the edges. Using a fork, make about 5-6 holes in the top of the piecrust, to let the steam escape. Bake in a 350° oven until edges are brown (about 35 minutes).

## PEANUT BUTTER TREATS

**2 cups peanut butter**

**2 cups graham cracker crumbs**

**1 cup confectioner's sugar**

**½ cup corn syrup – dark or light**

**¼ cup semi sweet chocolate chips, melted**

**colored sprinkles**

In large bowl, combine peanut butter, graham cracker crumbs, confectioner's sugar and corn syrup. Mix until smooth. Shape into 1-inch balls. Place on waxed paper. Drizzle melted chocolate over balls or roll in colored sprinkles.

Aa Bb Cc Dd Ee Ff Gg Hh Ii Jj Kk Ll Mm Nn Oo Pp

## AUNT EM'S TEA CAKES

3 eggs
1 cup oil
1 cup sugar
2 ½ cups self rising flour
1 teaspoon vanilla

Preheat oven to 350°. Mix all ingredients. Drop by teaspoonfuls onto greased cookie sheets. Bake in a 350° oven for 8-10 minutes.

These are irresistible. You can't eat just one!

## CHESS PIE

1 ½ cups sugar
3 eggs
1 teaspoon corn meal
1 teaspoon vinegar
1 stick butter
1 teaspoon vanilla

Preheat oven to 300°. Mix all ingredients. Bake in a 9-inch unbaked pie shell for 45 minutes.

## PECAN PIE

Eggs
1 cup Kao light syrup
1 cup sugar
2 tablespoons vanilla extract
1/8 teaspoon salt
1 cup pecan halves
Unbaked pastry shell

Preheat oven to 350°. In medium bowl, beat eggs slightly. Beat in next five ingredients. Stir in pecans. Pour into piecrust. Bake for 45-55 minutes, or until a knife inserted in the center comes out clean.

*Tip:* To keep your piecrust from burning while your pie cooks, wrap the edge of the piecrust in foil.

Qq  Rr  Ss  Tt  Uu  Vv  Ww  Xx  Yy  Zz    1 2 3 4 5 6 7 8 9 10

## CAKE SQUARES

1 box yellow cake mix

1 stick butter

1 egg

1 box confectioner's sugar

2 eggs

1 package cream cheese, softened

Preheat oven to 350°. In a large mixing bowl, combine cake mix, butter and 1 egg. Pour into greased 13 × 9 inch baking pan. In a medium mixing bowl, combine sugar, 2 eggs and cream cheese until smooth. Pour over cake mixture. Bake for 45 minutes, or until a toothpick inserted into the middle of cake comes out clean. Cool and cut into square.

## BROWNIES GALORE

1 cup sugar

3 tablespoons cocoa

2 eggs, beaten

1 teaspoon vanilla

¾ cup flour

1 stick butter

Preheat oven to 350°. Mix all ingredients. Pour into greased 9-inch square baking pan. Bake for 30 minutes. Cool and cut into squares.

## DROP MACAROONS

2 ½ cups flaked coconut

²/₃ cup semi sweet chocolate chips

²/₃ cups condensed milk

1 teaspoon vanilla

Preheat oven to 350°. Mix all ingredients until well blended. Drop by teaspoons onto greased cookie sheet. Bake 10-15 minutes in a 350° oven. Let cool before serving.

Aa Bb Cc Dd Ee Ff Gg Hh Ii Jj Kk Ll Mm Nn Oo Pp

## EASY CANDY BAR CAKE

1 box German chocolate cake mix

1 can (14 ounce) sweetened-condensed milk

1 12-ounce jar butterscotch topping

1 carton prepared whipped topping

3 crushed Heath Bars

Prepare cake according to package directions. Bake in a 13 x 9 inch pan. While cake is hot, poke holes in the top and pour milk over cake. Pour butterscotch topping over cake. Spread cake with whipped topping and sprinkle crushed Heath Bars over the top. Serve warm or can be refrigerated and served cold.

## COCONUT BARS

24 graham cracker squares, crushed

1 cup semi sweet chocolate chips

1 cup flaked coconut

¾ cup walnuts, chopped

1 can (14 ounce) sweetened condensed milk

Preheat oven to 350°. Combine crushed cracker crumbs, chocolate chips, coconut and walnuts, blending well. Add milk and stir. Spread batter into a greased 13 x 9 inch baking pan. Bake 15-20 minutes or until edges are golden brown. Cool and cut into bars.

## PUMPKIN CAKE

2 cups sugar

4 eggs

1-½ cups oil

3 cups flour

1 teaspoon cinnamon

1 cup walnuts

2 cups canned pumpkin

1 can prepared cream cheese frosting

Cream sugar, eggs and oil. Add flour and cinnamon. Blend well, but do not overmix. Add walnuts and pumpkin. Pour into greased and floured tube pan. Bake at 375° for 1 hour, or until toothpick inserted into the center comes out clean. Melt cream cheese frosting and pour over cake.

Qq  Rr  Ss  Tt  Uu  Vv  Ww  Xx  Yy  Zz    1 2 3 4 5 6 7 8 9 10

## NO COOK FONDANT

**⅓ cup margarine**

**⅓ cup light corn syrup**

**1 teaspoon vanilla**

**½ teaspoon salt**

**1 box (16 ounces)
confectioner's sugar**

In a large bowl, mix the first four ingredients until smooth. Add sugar all at once; mix first with a spoon, then with your hands. Turn out onto a board and knead until well blended and smooth. Shape as desired. Store in a cool place.

*Alternate:*

Nut creams: Shape dough into ½ inch balls. Press between 2 walnut or pecan halves.

Mocha logs: To syrup mixture, add 2 teaspoons instand coffee that has been dissolved in 1 teaspoon hot water. Shape into rolls about 2" long and ½" thick. Roll in chocolate sprinkles.

## PUMPKIN PIE

**1 (29-ounce) can pumpkin**

**2 (14-ounce) cans sweetened,
condensed milk**

**4 eggs**

**2 teaspoons cinnamon**

**9-inch unbaked pie shell,
2 piece**

**whipped topping (optional)**

**vanilla ice ream (optional)**

Preheat oven to 350°. Mix all ingredients until well blended. Pour into pie shells. This makes 2 pies. Bake about 45 minutes, or until knife inserted into center of pie comes out clean. Cool and top with whipped topping or vanilla ice cream.

Aa Bb Cc Dd Ee Ff Gg Hh Ii Jj Kk Ll Mm Nn Oo Pp

## PEANUT BUTTER LOAF

2 cups flour

4 teaspoons baking powder

1 teaspoon salt

²/₃ cup peanut butter

½ cup sugar

1 cup milk

Preheat oven to 425°. In a large mixing bowl, sift flour, baking powder and salt. In a small bowl, blend peanut butter and sugar. Add to dry ingredients with finger tips. Add milk to mixture. Mix well. Pour into well greased loaf pan. Bake at 425° for 35 minutes.

## MICROWAVE PEANUT BUTTER BARS

8-10 chocolate bars

1 cup peanut butter

2 sticks margarine, melted

1 box confectioner's sugar

2 cups graham cracker crumbs

Microwave chocolate bars until melted. Place all ingredients, except melted chocolate, into a mixing bowl. Mix and knead into an even mixture. Press mixture onto a deep cooking sheet, completely covering the bottom. Spread melted chocolate on top of mixture. Refrigerate. When cool, cut into small pieces.

## PEANUT BUTTER KISSES

1 cup peanut butter

1 cup light brown sugar, packed

1 egg

1 package chocolate kisses

Preheat oven to 350°. Mix peanut butter, sugar and egg until smooth. Shape into 1-½ inch balls. Place chocolate kiss in the middle of each ball. Bake 10-12 minutes. Cool completely. May substitute pecan halves for chocolate kiss.

## YUM YUM CAKE

1 box yellow cake mix

1 cup cold milk

1 small box vanilla instant
    pudding

8 ounces cream cheese

1 can crushed pineapple,
    (packed in water), undrained

1 carton whipped topping

coconut

pecans

**P**repare cake according to package directions. Let cool. Blend milk and pudding. Add cream cheese and blend well. Spread mixture on top of cooled cake. Top with pineapple, then whipped topping, then coconut, then pecans.

## CHEESE SQUARES

**First Layer:**

1 box butter cake mix

1 egg

1 stick butter, softened


**Second Layer:**

8 ounces cream cheese,
    softened

2 eggs

1 box confectioner's sugar

**P**reheat oven to 350°. First Layer: Mix dry cake mix with egg and butter; pour into 3 quart rectangular glass dish. Second layer: In a small mixing bowl, mix cream cheese, eggs and powdered sugar. Pour cream cheese mixture over first layer. Bake in a 350° oven for 50 minutes. Cut into squares.

Aa Bb Cc Dd Ee Ff Gg Hh Ii Jj Kk Ll Mm Nn Oo Pp

## CHOCOLATE CHIP POUND CAKE

¼ cup water

1 package butter cake mix

1 cup oil

8 ounce package of sour cream

1 package instant chocolate
   pudding mix

4 eggs

8 ounce package of chocolate
   chips

Preheat oven to 350°. Mix all ingredients; pour into grease tube pan. Bake in a 350° oven for 30-40 minutes.

## THANKSGIVING PUNCH

1 3-ounce package cherry
   gelatin

1 cup boiling water

1 (6-ounce) can frozen orange
   juice concentrate

3 cups cold water

1 quart cranberry juice cocktail
   (chilled)

1 12-ounce bottle ginger ale
   (chilled)

1 pint fruit flavored sherbet

Dissolve gelatin in boiling water. Stir in orange juice. Add cold water and cranberry juice cocktail. Place in a large punch bowl, add ice cubes. Slowly add chilled ginger ale. Add sherbet and stir. Yield: approximately 20 small glasses.

GOOP

(My sister-in-law, Anne Marie, gave this recipe to me.
She uses it for Bunco games or for church events.)

**2 pounds ground beef**

**1 can chili**

**1 pound velveeta cheese**

**1 can Rotel tomatoes**

**1 can ranch style beans**

**1 pint whipping cream**

Brown ground beef and drain. Return to pan and combine all other ingredients. Simmer until cheese melts and all ingredients are heated. Serve warm with tortilla chips.

## BLUE MOUNTAIN HUNT SCONES

My husband went to Utah on a hunting trip and came back
with this recipe. He absolutely loves it. Kurt and Tamra Lewis
spoiled him at their hunting camp.

**Scones:**

**Frozen Bread Dough – the kind that comes in a roll**

**Vegetable oil**

**Honey Butter Topping:**

**1 cup honey**

**1 stick butter, softened**

**2/3 cups powdered sugar**

Scones: Roll dough into long rectangle and cut into strips. Fry in hot vegetable oil. Turn with tongs as the strips become brown. Drain on paper towels.

Honey Butter: Mix honey butter and sugar and pour over hot scones. Can be used as a topping for cornbread, regular rolls or bread.